ALIve

BY GRACE

A ROADMAP TO HEALING

TOYIN TAIWO

Books may be purchased by contacting the Author and Publisher at:

publisher@exousiacreations.co.uk
Cover Design: Hadar Creations
Interior Design: Hadar Creations
Publishing Consultant: Hadar Creations
Publisher: Exousia Creations
Editors:
Ngozi Nzokurum
Nihinlola Latona
ISBN: 978-1-7399917-1-5

CONTENTS

FOREWORD.. 6

DEDICATION... 7

ACKNOWLEDGEMENT 8

PROLOGUE... 10

   MY STORY 10

SECTION ONE 14

CHAPTER 1 16

   IT IS HIS WILL 16

CHAPTER 2 20

GUARD YOUR HEART: AGAINST THE FEAR

OF DEATH.. 20

SECTION TWO 25

CHAPTER 3 27

  KNOW THE SOURCE... 27

CHAPTER 4 35

  INQUIRING OF THE LORD 35

CHAPTER 5 42

  RAISE PRAYER ALTARS.................................... 42

CHAPTER 6 52

  KEEP THE FAITH 52

CHAPTER 7 58

  BE SENSIBLE; TAKE CARE OF YOU 58

CHAPTER 8 66

  HE HEALED ME "LITTLE BY LITTLE" 66

SECTION THREE.. 74

CHAPTER 9 76

LIFE IN THE TONGUE 76

CHAPTER 10 78

MAINTAIN YOUR HEALING 78

CHAPTER 11 87

AND THEN SOME…… 87

HEALING SCRIPTURES 87

EPILOGUE 91

ABOUT THE AUTHOR 93

OTHER BOOKS 96

BIBLIOGRAPHY 99

NOTES 100

FOREWORD

Alive By Grace by Pastor Toyin Taiwo has pulled back the curtain to provide a detailed, intimate account of how she dealt with a very serious and life-threatening medical condition.

Along the way, we see how a deeply devoted disciple of Jesus reflects deeply on illness and healing with both realism about the facts, and trust in her Lord. Because of her many years of Biblical study, this book is rich with scriptural references that anchor her personal story in the Word of God, and it helps us to do the same.

Whether you are wrestling with your own health concerns or wish to encourage a friend, this book will stir up your faith, encourage your heart, and inform your mind.

Rev Dr Rick Lewis
Mentor, consultant and author of 'Mentoring Matters

DEDICATION

I dedicate this book to my Saviour, Redeemer, Author and the Finisher of my faith. He is the Bishop of my soul, Helper and the Lifter up of my head. My Love and my Life, who loves me enough to die for me, and has graciously called and anointed me despite who I am.

Your Majesty, I can only bow – I live to serve You.

ACKNOWLEDGEMENT

I want to thank the Almighty God who saved me by His power and has sustained me till today. I thank God for making my life an epitome of grace; nothing deserved, nothing earned, nothing qualified for, yet he works daily in my life.

I thank God for the people He puts in my life over the last four (4) decades of my journey in the Lord: especially Pastors Musa and Eunice Bako, and Pastors Bioye and Biodun Segun who have stood with me in prayer during the difficult months.

I want to thank my mentor, Rick Lewis, whom the Lord has used to discover and activate the gifts and inner treasures deposited in me; and has been a great support system to the church I was graced to oversee.

God used you to stabilize me and keep my focus on my divine assignment during a very difficult time of sickness - I appreciate you.

I'm also grateful to the leaders and members of Grace Chapel (RCCG) Chesterfield. I am proud to be one of you and being your Pastor has been inspiring and blissful –You are the best

To the Leaders and members of the Encounter Prayerline – your labour of love in these past years is highly appreciated.

A big thank you to my children and Cheer leaders. Special thanks to my amiable and supportive husband, I enjoy the grace of doing life with you and I love you

Toyin Taiwo
December 2021

PROLOGUE

MY STORY

I woke up on the beautiful Friday summer morning of July 2019 and noticed a sharp pain in my chest; just under the bust on both sides and I was severely breathless. Based on the amount of pain I was in, I knew I needed to see a GP urgently.

After our morning prayers, I rang the surgery and miraculously, the receptionist transferred me to a General Practitioner (GP) after she asked for my reason for calling.

I have been using this Surgery for 15 years and this has never happened. I was also not aware of anyone who rang the surgery and was transferred directly to one of the GPs from reception.

As incredible as it may sound, my first contact with the surgery during this ordeal started with God's favour, the appointment was treated as a matter of urgency. Indeed, it was my set time to be favoured.

You will arise and have mercy on Zion; For the time to favor her, Yes, the set time, has come.
Psalm 102:13.(NKJV)

The GP asked me certain questions about the presenting symptoms and asked me to go to the Surgery, told the reception that she had been expecting me and walk straight to her consulting room. This was another unusual favour.

At the Surgery, the GP did the ECG twice within 15minutes apart and narrated her concern about a "T-wave inversion." I had no clue what this meant but I had the inclination that whatever that means coupled with the presenting symptoms, informed her decision to call the ambulance.

While still in her office she typed the letters to take to the Accident and Emergency (A&E) department which she gave to the paramedic that came for me. I was really surprised by her attention to detail and how she treated me, the time spent with me and the care given by this doctor was awesome; especially these days when you only get 10 minutes in your appointment with a GP.

The ambulance arrived and I was taken to A&E. Blood samples were taken and the first set of results confirmed the GP's diagnosis that I had "Pulmonary Embolism," that is, I had a clot in my lungs. Within minutes, I was given blood thinning injection while awaiting further investigation.

I was taken for an X-ray and eventually a CT-Scan and when the results came in, I noticed a palpable panic among the medical personnel (I've been trained in interpreting body languages and facial expressions), they had seen what they didn't expect in the scan but they wouldn't speak to me until a senior doctor came along.

Eventually, someone that I perceived to be a senior doctor told me that the CT scan revealed swollen lymph nodes all over my chest. This started a six-month long medical investigation that took me to the hospital almost every week, either for tests, scans or for consultations.

I was discharged that night after spending 12 hours in the hospital. I came out of the hospital emotionally numb; I didn't know what to think or say and I couldn't even pray.

This book is a record of what I experienced physically emotionally and spiritually and what I learnt during the six months of medical investigations, while I prayed and hoped for healing.

This experience eventually resulted in deeper divine encounters and relationship with God. May you be blessed as you read prayerfully and with rapt attention.

SECTION ONE

"Benefit of Redemption"

Healing is one of the benefit of our redemption! Jesus died and rose again for our sins, but much more than this, He died and rose again for our sicknesses and diseases too. Healing belongs to us just as salvation belongs to us. Healing is part and parcel of our redemption!

".......forget not all his benefits: who forgives all your sins and heals all your diseases, **Psalm 103:2b-3 (NIV)**

The Lord heals all our diseases . . . not just a few, and not just the minor ailments. Nothing is left out of the work of redemption completed by Christ: not a headache and not any kind of cancer.

14

Healing in our physical bodies is supposed to be a normal part of life for followers of Jesus. Guard your heart from fear; It is His will to Heal you.

CHAPTER 1

IT IS HIS WILL

Is my healing God's will? Will He heal me completely? Has healing ceased with the apostles?

I believe the word of God that says, *"…by His stripes you were healed"* – **1 Peter 2:24 (NKJV)**. If you know the Lord and have a personal relationship with Him and you are saved, you can be healed. The grace that brought salvation to us, brought healing with it.

I came back home from the hospital with my mind flooded with all the reports from the scan and X-ray asking God if it was His will to heal me. **Friends, it is always His will.**

Supernatural healing in our physical bodies is supposed to be a normal part of life for followers of Jesus. Every Christian can minister healing. You don't have to be the leader of a church, God can use you wherever you are, whether you're at church, at home, or anywhere in the world.

I have heard people say that it may not be God's will for them to be healed. This is a question that has been asked for ages and we also see an example of this in *Matthew 8:2(NIV)* when the leprous man asked Jesus *"Lord, if you are willing"* and Jesus answered directly with a simple answer saying *"I am willing."*

God is willing to heal. He wants to heal all manner of sicknesses and diseases.

If He was willing in the past, He is still willing now. *"Jesus Christ is the same yesterday and today and forever." Hebrews 13:8 (NIV).*

When we look at the healing ministry of Jesus we see in **Matthew 8:2** that it is His will to heal us. We also see in *Matthew 8: 16*(NKJV) that ...*He healed ALL who were sick.*

Jesus was motivated by compassion to heal and he always healed them ALL by the word, He had a healing ministry and He used the gifts of the Holy Spirit.

He healed people even from a distance and Jesus said, *"Greater works shall you do"* **John 14:12**. So Jesus will heal through our prayers, founded on His word, which is a further revelation of the fact that it is His will to heal.

Healing miracles are still happening today, and I am a living witness to this.

He will heal if we don't doubt or let the lies of the devil deceive us.

God says, *"Healing is the children's bread"* **Mark 7:27.** If this is so, why am I sick?

Firstly, I want you to know that ownership and possession is not the same. You could have been willed a property as a child but will not take possession of it until you become an adult legally. (**Galatians. 4:1).**

Healing is not a promise in the New Covenant. A promise is something that has not yet been done. A promise has to do with the future. But healing is something that has already been bought and paid for and is now yours through the sacrifice of Jesus Christ.

God has already done something about sickness and disease. Now, we are supposed to do something; we are to resist sickness and actively receive and possess it by faith, which is the healing God has already given us in Christ.

God told the children of Israel in the Old Testament that the Promised Land belonged to them, however, it was still occupied by giants and they had to fight to possess the land. Provision has been made by God for the possession of good and godly gift which includes our healing, for this reason **1 Peter 2:24** says, *"by His stripes we were healed."*

CHAPTER 2

GUARD YOUR HEART: AGAINST THE FEAR OF DEATH

Above all else, guard your heart, for everything you do flows from it. Keep your mouth free of perversity; keep corrupt talk far from your lips. Let your eyes look straight ahead; fix your gaze directly before you. Give careful thought to the paths for your feet and be steadfast in all your ways. Do not turn to the right or the left; keep your foot from evil. **Proverbs 4:23-27 (NIV)**

I was booked to see the consultant at the respiratory department. The Doctors did not give a specific diagnosis at this point but mentioned that several lymph nodes in my chest were swollen.

During the consultations, I gathered that I was being investigated for lung cancer, tuberculosis, and pulmonary sarcoidosis.

I went back home anxious and confused, I began to ask myself, "Is it my time to go home?" I was terrified by all the information I had just received; the enemy attacked my mind with fear. Fear of what was going to happen and the fear of death. Fear of how my children would cope, fear of the impact on my aged mother, fear of leaving the church behind, etc.

A few years ago, I had read the book, "Battlefield of the mind" but that time I was experiencing a very fierce battle in my mind. Despite, I remembered reading about "Mind binding Spirits", my mind was jammed, it couldn't function properly; fear crippled and tormented me. My mind was attacked, and I began to fear death. I was terrified for days despite knowing that I am a pilgrim on this earth and would be going home at some point.

I knew I needed to change my thoughts. I had to fight against the thought of why God allowed it! What I did wrong? Or perhaps I sinned and that's why I was sick? I was flooded with further thoughts of, "What if I become sicker and I can't do things for myself? What if I die?

My mind was attacked with doubts about my recovery and my healing. I was enveloped with new but wrong interpretations of God's sovereignty that excludes His love.

My mind was attacked with unbelief which grew for a short while. My Spirit sank and I can't quite say if I was depressed or not, but I was anxious about the situation; not knowing exactly what it was and whether it was a treatable condition or not.

In my distress, I was reminded of the scripture that says, "*As a man thinketh in his heart, so is he*" **(Proverbs 23:7 - KJV)**. Your thoughts; positive or negative, good or bad, control your attitude. Your attitude is the sum total of your thoughts. Your attitude leads to your actions.

I decided to begin to be conscious of what I was thinking about. I knew I had to regain control of my mind to find peace and freedom.

I recalled what I had read in inspirational books, I started giving myself empowering self-talks, I told myself repeatedly:

"Think positive thoughts and meditate on the word of God. Hide the word of God in your heart. It is the word of God that renews the mind and weakens the attack of the enemy on the mind."

I began to confess the word of God in *John 8:31-32(NKJV)* **and** *Psalms 107:20(NKJV)* which respectively say that *"If I abide in God's word, I will know the truth and the truth shall make me free"* and *"He sent His word and healed them, and delivered them from their destructions"*. I started declaring that the word of God will heal me.

I also meditated on the scripture in **Philippians 4:6-7(NKJV)**: *Be anxious for nothing, but in everything by prayer and supplication, with* *thanksgiving, let your requests be made known to God; and the peace of God, which surpasses all understanding, will guard your hearts and minds through Christ Jesus.*

I turned to prayers and thanksgiving with the understanding that thanksgiving is a sentry that guards against anxiety and worry.

Also, I was instructed from **Proverbs 4:23-27**, to

- Govern my speech **(v. 24)**

- Guard my sight **(v. 25)**

- Guide my steps **(v. 27)**

I confessed scriptures daily and meditated on them and prayed with thanksgiving. The result was that I began to experience the grace of God and faith arose within me (some of these healing scriptures are written in the later part of this book).

SECTION TWO

"Receiving My Healing"

God heals instantly and sometimes He heals gradually in stages. Receiving healing is a process. In **Mark 10:51-52.** We see God heal the blind man instantly while in **Mark 8:22-26,** He healed the blind man in stages and progressively.

In *John 9:1-8(NKJV),* we saw that Jesus, *"...spat on the ground, made clay with the saliva; and He anointed the eyes of the blind man with the clay. And He said to him, "Go, wash in the pool of Siloam" (which is translated, Sent). So he went and washed, and came back seeing"*.

But in Mark 8, He didn't touch the blind man, He only spoke. He said, *"Your faith has made you whole."*

The Lord graciously took me through the process of my healing that I may gain understanding and strengthen others. He spoke to me from **Isaiah 35:3-4(NKJV).** which says *Strengthen the weak hands, And make firm the feeble knees. Say to those who are fearful-hearted, "Be strong, do not fear! Behold, your God will come with vengeance, With the recompense of God; He will come and save you."*

God is not limited in methods or power, He is a sovereign God and heals as He wills.

The road to my healing as taught by the Lord is explained in the acronym below:

K - Know the source

I - Inquire of the Lord

R - Raise prayer altars

K - Keep the faith

These are explained in the next four chapters.

CHAPTER 3

KNOW THE SOURCE

Sickness is not of God, this is why Jesus went about healing the sick. **Mark 4:23**

It is an error to think that God afflicts with sicknesses. However, God may allow the devil in order that we will grow and to use every situation to bring about His glory and make all things work together for good to those who love him.

Sicknesses arise from different sources, some of which will be discussed in this chapter. Let's have a look:

1. Sin

Sickness is a consequence of the original sin of Adam and Eve.

In fact, the Bible tells us how sickness originated. We find that all illnesses and ailments came about as a result of the initial sin of Adam and Eve in the Garden of Eden.

Sin is to life what rust is to metal. It eats away, tarnishes, devalues, and prevents you from fulfilling your purpose.

The Scriptures reveal that Jesus healed in the bible by simply saying "your sins are forgiven." Sin is in the foundation of all evil.

In **Mark 2: 3-12,** a paralytic man was brought to Jesus and let into the house through the roof. Jesus saw the faith of the friends of this man and said to him in **verse 5**, *".... your sins are forgiven"*

Adam and Eve were told that the death process would begin if they disobeyed God. Sickness is part of that process. If we engage in unconfessed and wilful sins, we open up ourselves to death and accelerate its process, our bodies degenerate and eventually dies. Sin gives the enemy a legal ground to afflict us with diseases.

During the week when all the medical investigations commenced, the Holy Spirit led me into a time of self-examination. I started confessing my sins and repenting of them as the Holy Spirit brought them to my memory. I was even surprised at some of the things I recalled, confessed and asked God's forgiveness and cleansing for.

In **John 14:30(NKJV)**, Jesus said that, "....*the ruler of this world is coming and has nothing in me*", that is, the devil has no legal claim (authority, control) over Christ.

The devil has authority and control over the kingdom of the world **(Luke 4:5-6)** and over the non-Christians **(John 8:43-44)** but has no authority over Christ because Christ committed no sin.

As I received confidence in the place of prayer and was refreshed knowing that the accuser of the brethren had nothing on me; I got my first release from this repentance and confession of sins

2. The Activities of the devil

The second source of sickness to look into, is the activities of the devil

In *Luke 13:16(NKJV) So ought not this woman, being a daughter of Abraham, whom Satan has bound – think of it – for eighteen years, be loosed from this bond on the Sabbath?"*

This woman was sick for 18 years and was bent over, could not stand straight but Jesus said, SHE WAS BOUND BY THE DEVIL. It is therefore important to know the source of your sickness in order to address it appropriately.

A REVELATION

On a certain day, before my next appointment with the consultant, I remembered that two years prior to this sudden occurrence, I had a revelation where I was touched with a stick and all the organs in my body began to turn to ash.

In this revelation, I began to plead the blood of Jesus. As I did this, my organs began to change back to normal colour from my lower abdomen towards my chest until there was only a portion under my rib cage and I was startled out of this revelation.

On the day I was told that there was a shadow on my lungs, I remembered this revelation. I realised that this disease was not physical or natural, IT WAS AN ATTACK FROM THE ENEMY.

As one who has ministered deliverance prayers for two decades, I knew I needed God's deliverance from this attack and its effect.

I took a train to London to visit my friend; Veronica Good-God, who prayed deliverance prayers over me with her mum.

I came out of her house three hours later, felt like a heavy load was lifted off my shoulders and the fear of death was gone. I went home with inexplicable joy in heart. All the residual doubt I had, left me.

It is imperative to note here that surrounding yourself with spiritually sensitive friends who are ready to intercede at the prompting of the Holy Spirit is very advisable in our life's journey.

3.   Congenital Birth Defects

Some people are born with sicknesses and diseases in their bodies (naturally) and even mentally.

As He passed along, He noticed a man blind from his birth. His disciples asked Him, Rabbi, who sinned, this man or his parents, that he should be born blind? Jesus answered, It was not that this man or his parents sinned, but he was born blind in order that the workings of God should be manifested (displayed and illustrated) in him.

John 9:1-3 (AMPC)

In this scripture, we see a birth defect in a man (blind from birth).

The sin of Adam set the principle of death and its associated destruction in the world and we have had to deal with it ever since; children being born with defects and disabilities, is also as a result of this.

Jesus said that this sickness was not as a result of any sin of either parent or the sick man, but a birth defect which has its root in the fall of Adam.

God wants to work in and through every congenital disease and every other sickness as he did in my case.

God may reveal His works in other lives, in other ways; such as joy and endurance in the midst of the difficulty. It is in conquering and abolishing evil that the name of God is glorified.

In the economy of God's providence, the blind man's suffering in the Scripture above had its place and aim, and this was to glorify God as he was to be healed by the Redeemer.

God overruled the disaster of the child's blindness so that, when the child grew to manhood, he would, by the recovering of his sight, see the glory of God in the face of Christ and others. Consequently seeing the works of God might turn him to the true Light of the World.

CHAPTER 4

INQUIRING OF THE LORD

Inquiring of the Lord means asking for information, revelation or insight from the Lord in different situations including health aspect.

During the following week, after I was admitted and discharged from the Accident & Emergency department, I received grace to inquire from the Lord about my health and healing.

As I had been delivered from the fear of death, I began to inquire of the Lord as to whether it was my time to come home?"

During the days of inquiring from the Lord and self-examination, I was led into prayers of repentance to ensure that sin had not brought me into the situation I was in. This was done so as to eliminate its hold in my life.

I sought the Lord as enabled by His Spirit until I had complete peace in my heart and knew that the enemy would find nothing in me. I was ushered into a season of refreshing and intimacy with God.

The Lord spoke to me from this scripture:

According to my earnest expectation and hope that in nothing I shall be ashamed, but with all boldness, as always, so now also Christ will be magnified in my body, whether by life or by death. For to me, to live is Christ, and to die is gain.

But if I live on in the flesh, this will mean fruit from my labor; yet what I shall choose I cannot tell. For I am hard-pressed between the two, having a desire to depart and be with Christ, which is far better.

Nevertheless to remain in the flesh is more needful for you. And being confident of this, I know that I shall remain and continue with you all for your progress and joy of faith, that your rejoicing *for me may be more abundant in Jesus Christ by my coming to you again. **Philippians 1:20-26(NKJV)***

I was in a time and season of refreshing and sweet fellowship with the Lord, I felt like there was nothing to hang on to in this world. On one hand, I desired to see my grandchildren, I wanted to see our church continue to fulfil its mission in our town, I wanted to watch the new converts grow and blossom in the Lord.

I have prayed for and desired to see revival in our town but on the other hand, where I was with the Lord was so sweet that I felt like going home where there is no pain, no sickness and no suffering.

The Scripture, *"For to me, to live is Christ, and to die is gain,"* became real to me. I experienced the reality of what Paul highlighted in the scripture above especially in verse 23, *"For I am hard-pressed between the two, having a desire to depart and be with Christ, which is far better."*

However, the Lord God, in answering my questions, began to ask me questions about what he had told me in the past. The promises He had made and the assignment he had given to me. He asked if they were fulfilled and if the assignment looked completed to me.

The answer was NO! So, I understood that this was not the will of God and that I had to fight for my health in order to complete my course.

It changed my attitude towards the situation. Knowing that it was not God's time or will for me to die. I arose from the bed of oppression that bound me through fear. Then, I began to address the infirmity.

The importance of my health was clear to me, especially if I am to be used for the cause of the gospel and to finish the course.

From that moment, I went into the hospitals for all the investigations, consultations and procedures without fear.

It is scriptural for you to enquire of the Lord, and He always answers.

We can see from the precious illustration in John chapter 9 about the nature of the blind man situation. The disciples were actually inquiring from the Lord to know the source or cause of the blindness.

WHY INQUIRE?

When we inquire of the Lord, we are at an advantage because of the following reasons:

1. The Lord reveals the state of our hearts and of our lives to us. We see in **Joshua 7:10-12**, when Joshua inquired of the Lord to know why they were defeated by a small army at Ai, God revealed that there was sin in the camp. By this inquiry, the situation was dealt with.

2. He gives us **inside information** and an edge in the situation. In **1 Samuel 10:22-23(NKJV),** the children of Israel inquired of the Lord, *"...Has the man come here yet?" And the Lord answered, "There he is, hidden among the equipment."*

3. To know God's will - **James 4:3a(NKJV)** says *"You ask and do not receive, because you ask amiss."* Knowing the will of God will inform your prayers. It enables you to pray aright and according to God's will.

4. We receive **Peace** and **Confidence** to continue to trust. When you inquire of the Lord and He answers you, you receive peace. It floods your soul, and you are kept in perfect peace because your heart is stayed on Him **(Isaiah 26:3)**

5. We receive **guidance and battle strategies. 2 Chronicles 20:3;** Jehoshaphat inquired of the Lord concerning the battle with the three nations that came together against him to battle. And God gave him a battle strategy to put musicians and singers in front and the physical weapons behind and the Lord fought the battle on their behalf.

6. **Victory (Success)** is assured. **1 Samuel 30:8, 18-20. & 1 Samuel 23:1-13**. David inquired of the Lord if he should pursue the enemies to retrieve all that had been

stolen. In **1 Samuel 23:1-13(NKJV)** David inquired of the Lord and God said in verse 4b "…*Arise, go down to Keilah. For I will deliver the Philistines into your hand.*"

CHAPTER 5

RAISE PRAYER ALTARS

An altar can be simply defined as a place of sacrifice, worship, consecration, it can be a physical location like a temple or even a human temple which is our bodies. Further definitions are:

- A meeting point between human and spirit beings.
- A place where covenants are cut and vows are made.
- A gate into the spirit world to make way for angelic traffic.

Raising an altar of godly prayer simply means creating a meeting place between you and God or between others and God.

There are types of Prayer Altar as highlighted below:

1.   Personal Prayer Altar

It means being intentional about spending quality time in that space; physically and spiritually.

In doing this, you are participating in an act of worship. By going into that place, you are able to present yourself to God and offer up your life to him each and every day.

I appeal to you therefore, brothers, by the mercies of God, to present your bodies as a living sacrifice, holy and acceptable to God, which is your spiritual worship. **Romans 12:1 ESV**

When you have made that commitment to go to your secret place with a humble heart, be ready to hear from God, stay in the Word. Ensure to sit in silence and listen to his voice, wait for him till He speaks and you're aware of His presence. This way, you are building your Prayer Altar

We see an example of a king in the Old Testament who was seriously sick unto death.

He was told by the prophet to put his house in order as he was going to die.

> *In those days Hezekiah became deadly ill. The prophet Isaiah son of Amoz came and said to him, Thus says the Lord: Set your house in order, for you shall die; you shall not recover.*

> *Then Hezekiah turned his face to the wall and prayed to the Lord, saying, "I beseech You, O Lord, [earnestly] remember now how I have walked before You in faithfulness and truth and with a whole heart [entirely devoted to You] and have done what is good in Your sight. And Hezekiah wept bitterly.*

> *Before Isaiah had gone out of the middle court, the word of the Lord came to him: "Turn back and tell Hezekiah, the leader of My people, Thus says the Lord, the God of David your [forefather]: I have heard your prayer, I have seen your tears; behold, I will heal you. On the third day you shall go up to the house of the Lord.*

> *I will add to your life fifteen years and deliver you and this city [Jerusalem] out of the hand*

of the king of Assyria; and I will defend this city for My own sake and for My servant David's sake.

2 Kings 20:1-6(ESV)

On hearing the word of the Lord, Hezekiah faced the wall and prayed to God, putting God in remembrance of how he had walked before Him in faithfulness, truthfulness, wholehearted devotion, and also narrated his goodness in God's sight.

Hezekiah presented his case and you must do same. He prayed to God for a healing and God answered him. No matter how you feel, you must have a personal altar where you raise prayers unto the Lord daily about your life's (which includes your health) condition.

Every day, the spirit of God chose particular healing scriptures for me to pray with and I prayed with these scriptures daily in obedience.

2. Corporate Prayer Altar

The importance of corporate prayers cannot be over-emphasized. *"one man will chase a thousand and two put ten thousand to flight."* **Deuteronomy 32:30(NIV)**.

We are stronger together. Whatever is not dealt with at the personal altar can be dealt with on the corporate altar because we have different graces, unction and anointing.

"Again I say to you that if two of you agree on earth concerning anything that they ask, it will be done for them by My Father in heaven. For where two or three are gathered together in My name, I am there in the midst of them."
Matthew 18:19-20(NKJV)

The Deaconry (Deacons and Deaconesses) in our church and Prayer Partners on the Encounter Prayerline raised corporate prayer altars. They prayed daily throughout the whole period of the medical investigations.

They interceded and did spiritual warfare. They prayed all manner of prayers and God in His infinite mercy, answered them. There has been no time that I had felt so blessed that I am in the body of Christ, than in that phase of my life.

Knowing that whether I was present or not, a prayer altar has been raised in my name and the brethren are constantly interceding for me.

James 5:16a (NKJV) says *"Confess your faults one to another, and pray one for another, that ye may be healed. The effectual fervent prayer of a righteous man avails much."*

I saw the performance of this scripture in my life as the brethren prayed for me. Indeed the prayer of the saints avails much and I was healed. Halleluiah!

3. Submit to deliverance prayers (Altars of other ministers)

Deliverance can be a confusing and questionable subject for some Christians especially because of how it is conducted. However, we saw Jesus deliver people throughout His earthly ministry and also we can rest in the fact that God's Word clearly defines the existence of Satan, evil spirits, and their attempts to disrupt our lives.

Our Lord Jesus Christ dealt directly with Satan himself; not only in the spiritual realm as he faced death on the cross, but before that in the physical realm when Satan tempted him in the wilderness **(Matt. 4: 1–13, Mark 1:13, Luke 4:1–15).**

The enemy waited until Jesus was weakened in His physical body, having fasted 40 days, and then tempted Him. If Jesus had given in to Satan and sinned, He would no longer have been able to fulfil the role His Father had created for Him: to die for us - the perfect sacrifice for all mankind.

Jesus resisted the temptations of the evil one, and this account of His confrontation with Satan serve not to only prove His perfect purity and sinless nature, but also the real existence of Satan and its activities.

1 John 3:8(NIV) tells us, *"The reason the Son of God appeared was to destroy the devil's work."* Jesus not only cast out demons as part of His work on earth, as is evidenced throughout the Gospels, but He taught about Satan and his demons.

"Then they brought to him a demoniac who was blind and mute; and he cured him, so that the one who had been mute could speak and see **(Matt 12:22)** – Jesus prayed deliverance prayers over him.

Deliverance prayer is one of the most powerful forms of prayer for healing (spiritual and physical healing). Once we recognise the existence of the evil one, we can step out in faith to destroy its power.

As Christians, we know that nothing happens in the physical that has not happened first in the spiritual. As deliverance prayers are prayed over you, every spiritual undertone connected to the sickness is dealt with and the healing manifests in the physical.

As written in Chapter 3 of this book, I had deliverance prayers prayed over me and felt the oppression of the enemy lifted from my life on that day.

4.   Prayers by your Elders/Leaders

Is any sick among you? let him call for the elders of the church; and let them pray over him, anointing him with oil in the name of the Lord: And the prayer of faith shall save the sick, and the Lord shall raise him up; and if he have committed sins, they shall be forgiven him. **James 5:14(NIV)**

It is a good thing for your brothers and sisters in Christ to pray with you, intercede on your behalf, and pray in agreement with you.

"Again, I say to you that if two of you agree on earth concerning anything that they ask, it will be done for them by My Father in heaven" - **Matthew 18:19(NKJV)**

Indeed, prayers by your elders, Church leaders and Pastors takes it to another level because of the authority that God gave them to watch over your soul. Every prayer that your leader prays over you, gets answered if you believe and do not despise them.

Even though I pastor a church by the grace of God, I also called on my leaders, for instance, the Pastors in charge of our Province and Region (oversees 50 Churches) to pray over me to establish that authority that the enemy cannot resist.

It is important as children of God to pay attention to divine protocol. This is because God will always perform the words of His prophets.

CHAPTER 6

KEEP THE FAITH

Keeping the faith is to continue to believe, trust, when it is difficult to do so.

Faith; according to **Hebrews 11:1(NKJV)** *is the substance of things hoped for and the evidence of things not seen.* It is what compels, drives, and assures us. It gives us conviction and confidence to keep holding on.

In the scripture above, after the author defined and described faith, he gave examples of people who lived by faith. When you look at the list, these people all had some things in common; every one of them swam against the current (turbulent situation) of their time.

Every one of them marched to the beat of a different drummer. Every one of them lived against the odds. They lived by a creed different from that of the world and each one made a difference for the kingdom of God.

Enoch walked with God against the odds. Noah built an ark when the sun was still shining. Sarah and Abraham gave birth to nations in their old age against. And Moses went to Egypt to tell Pharaoh, *"let my people go"*, in **Exodus 9:1** and led the Israelites out of Egypt."

Faith! This is the diet of the righteous. *"The righteous shall live by his faith."* **Habakkuk 2:4(ESV)**

Jesus said, "If you have faith like the size of a mustard seed you will say to this mountain be moved from here to there and it will obey you." (Matt 17:20)

Jesus healed many in scripture, saying, *"...your faith has made you whole."*

He told the woman with the issue of blood the same statement although this woman added works to her faith by ploughing through the vast crowd to get to Jesus and touched the hem of His garment.

Keep the faith by adding works to it. The work you add to your faith by letting your words and your actions align with your prayers and what you are believing God for.

Keep the faith! And that faith will keep you, because the source of faith is the Living God.

Back to my story - throughout the whole ordeal, and the changing diagnosis and investigations, the Lord kept speaking *"the just shall live by faith"* into my spirit.

I held on to the word of God as enabled by the Holy Spirit and reminded myself each day to keep the faith in the face of negative and contrary evidence.

You may still be experiencing pain or other symptoms, Keep the faith!

Faithful is He who has calls you, He also will do it. **1 Thessalonians 5:24(NASB)**

You must keep the faith to receive and keep your healing.

What do you do when you get a bad diagnosis? You keep the faith because the scripture says, *"The just shall live by faith"*.

What do you do when you are in pain? You believe that *"The just shall live by faith"*.

What do you do when the enemy tries to steal, kill and destroy? You keep the faith by declaring, *"The just shall live by faith"*.

What do you do when evildoers seem to have it all together? You keep echoing that, *"The just shall live by faith"*.

What do you do when your prayers seem to go unanswered? You believe that, *"The just shall live by faith"*.

What do you do when your dreams seem to turn to ashes? You proclaim that, *"The just shall live by faith"*.

When all you see is trouble on every hand, the righteous man remembers that God is still on His throne, and when the dark clouds break over his head, he says to himself, *"The just shall live by faith."*

You will not find rest for your soul until you understand that the just shall live by faith. God is in control; He rules and reigns in the affairs of men. He has power to do all things, and nothing is impossible with Him.

"For in it the righteousness of God is revealed from faith to faith; as it is written, "The just shall live by faith." **Romans 1:17(NKJV)**

We are to stand fast in the faith, be brave and be strong **(1 Corinthians 16:13)**.

We must remain steadfast, immovable, always abounding in the works of the Lord, knowing that your labour is not in vain in the Lord **(1 Corinthians 15:58)**.

No matter what you face, keep serving the Lord, keep loving the Lord and keep trusting in Him.

Hold tight!

Don't give up!

Don't let go!

Keep the faith and He will reward your faith!

CHAPTER 7

BE SENSIBLE; TAKE CARE OF YOU

As Christians, as we pray, apply our faith, and believe God for supernatural healing; it is also important that you take responsibility to have good health and take some physical steps to maintain it.

There is no evidence that God is opposed to medical or physical help in your healing process. It is lack of wisdom to refuse medical attention in the name of faith or to reject physical actions that can impact your health positively.

When He had said these things, He spat on the ground and made clay with the saliva; and He anointed the eyes of the blind man with the clay.
John 9:6 (NKJV)

In this scripture, Jesus found it important to change His method of healing so one could never make a formula of the methods or stereotype it. The power is in God to heal, not in a method.

God choses to heal with or without the use medicine. It is the reason why people took the same medications as others and they are not healed because the healing power is in God not dependent upon the method.

Let's use acronym, M.E.R.E. - to explain how we must take care of ourselves:

M- Medical Attention

E - Eat Well

R - Rest Well

E - Exercise Often

M - Medical Attention – Pay attention to the medical provisions available to you as it is one of the methods that God uses to heal.

"So he went to him and bandaged his wounds, pouring on oil and wine; and he set him on his own animal, brought him to an inn, and took care of him." **Luke 10:34 (NKJV)**

Here, we see the wounded man in the parable of the Good Samaritan, treated with medicine (oil, wine and bandages)

We should always seek help from God as well as going for appropriate medical treatment. In Matthew 9, the Pharisees asked Jesus why he spent time with sinners. He replied, '*It is not the healthy who need a doctor, but the sick*' **Matthew 9:12(NIV)**. Jesus recognised that sick people need doctors.

It is important that you attend all your medical appointments and do your medical checks and as well put your trust in God.

Eat well: It is important that we eat healthy and balanced meals. Daniel and the other three Hebrew boys refused the rich and luxurious food of the king but fed on healthy food that would not defile them and looked healthier than the rest of their peers upon examination after ten days **(Daniel 1:15).**

Some people ignorantly tend to eat large quantities of carbohydrate and less of other nutrients. This makes them put on weight which causes all manner of ill-health conditions.

Nowadays, we see that in the treatment of some sicknesses like diabetes, high blood pressure, fatty liver etc., doctors prescribe exercise, among other things, in the healing process.

I found that as I added more and more of vegetables and some protein and less of carbohydrates, I lost weight naturally and became healthier daily.

> *"… whether you eat or drink or whatever*
> *you do, do it all for the glory of God."*
> **1 Corinthians 10:31(NKJV).**

When you bring God into eating healthily, it changes everything. Striving to honour Him in your food and drink choices will bring about not only a change of heart, but it will also change your lifestyle.

> *"Just because something is technically legal*
> *doesn't mean that it's spiritually appropriate. If I*
> *went around doing whatever I thought I could get*
> *by with, I'd be a slave to my whims. You know the*
> *old saying, "First you eat to live, and then you live*
> *to eat"?*
>
> *Well, it may be true that the body is only a*
> *temporary thing, but that's no excuse for stuffing*
> *your body with food or indulging it with sex. Since*
> *the Master honours you with a body, honour him*
> *with your body!*

1 Corinthians 6:12(MSG)

In another words, this scripture says if you don't control your food appetite you become a slave to food.

Don't abuse your body, give it what is healthy and in the process, you will honour God who honoured you with a body in the first place.

Rest well: GOD rested after creating the whole word and prescribed rest for us in the Sabbath day.

In the creation account in the Book of Genesis, God spent the first six days working. On the seventh day, He set an example for humanity to imitate: He rested.

By the seventh day God had finished the work he had been doing; so on the seventh day he rested from all his work. Then God blessed the seventh day and made it holy, because on it he rested from all the work of creation that he had done. **Gen. 2:2-3 (NIV)**

If God who needed no rest, rested, we should also rest. The reason for the Sabbath was rest and even though we are no longer under the law, we must take at least a day out to rest. This is because our body becomes weak after working hard and needs to recharge.

We read about Jesus sleeping at the bottom of the boat, resting because his body needed to recharge.

Also, it is important to rest for a clear and good mental clarity and capacity because the things we say and the decisions we make when we are tired may not be the best.

Exercise often: Physical Therapists say that exercises has many benefits for your body and brain, such as:

- It improves your memory and brain function (all age groups)
- Prevents many chronic diseases
- Aids in weight management
- Lowers blood pressure
- Improve heart health

- Improves your quality of sleep
- Reduces feelings of anxiety and depression
- Combats cancer-related fatigue
- Relieves joint pain and stiffness
- Maintains muscle strength and balance; and
- May increase life span.

1 Timothy 4:8 ... *bodily exercise profits a little*

If we reap the "little" that bodily exercise brings and add it to the spiritual exercise of praying and studying the Word, we will have a holistic good health.

A lot of Christians have lost their lives simply because they did not pay attention to the physical care of their bodies. Be wise! Be Sensible.

CHAPTER 8

HE HEALED ME "LITTLE BY LITTLE"

A month after my first admission into A & E, during my personal devotion, the Lord said to me "you are going through an 'MOT' Certification process."

What does this mean?

The MOT (Ministry of Transport) test is an annual test of vehicle safety, roadworthiness aspects and exhaust emissions required in the United Kingdom for most vehicles over three years old.

When you take your car in for an MOT test, it will either pass or fail the test. If it fails, the garage will identify the faults and with your agreement, they repair, renew or replace parts. They will then run the test again to ensure it passes. Then they will give you a certificate stating it has passed and it is now "road worthy" for another year.

The Holy Spirit said to me, I am in the process of making you "road worthy" for another 10 years. As the days went by, I became progressively healed and I saw all symptoms gradually varnished.

"And the Lord your God will drive out those nations before you little by little; you will be unable to destroy them at once, lest the beasts of the field become too numerous for you. But the Lord your God will deliver them over to you, and will inflict defeat upon them until they are destroyed."
Deuteronomy 7:22-23(NKJV)

As the children of Israel were about to enter into the Promised Land, God said that He would drive out the enemies before them little by little so that the beasts of the field do not increase among them.

I believe that the beast referred to here, is "pride." Lest pride overcome me, the Lord healed me little by little and one body part after the other.

I went into the hospital with the diagnosis of "Pulmonary Embolism" which was confirmed by blood tests but was ruled out after further investigations and much prayers and declaration of the word of God.

Then I received letters to visit a clinic at the Macmillan section of the Royal Hospital to see a consultant. He looked at the CT scan on his computer and tried to explain what he could see. After several questions, he showed me the images on his screen saying that he was sending me to Sheffield Hospitals for a PET scan. He said that if the scan came back and the chest area he showed me, lighted up, it would mean there is cancer in my lungs.

The church prayed and declared the word of God again and a week later, I went for the PET scan. When the results came, I was called to the Royal Hospital Respiratory Department to discuss the results.

The consultant showed me the images on his screen and the area he had expressed concern about at the last appointment, had lighted up. "It is probably cancer of the lungs," he said. He asked me if I was a smoker, etc. He decided to do a biopsy to get samples from the lymph nodes.

The church began to pray with this information from the consultant, declaring the word!!! I got prayer support globally on the Encounter Prayerline, the Church Deaconry and the brethren.

The consultant later sent me home saying that I would receive a letter for the ultrasound procedure to get the samples. The attempt to take the samples under ultrasound failed, they couldn't get a viable sample so the consultant decided they would go in through my neck into my chest.

This procedure which was carried out in Sheffield Hospitals, was successful by the grace of God. When the results came back, there was no sign of lung cancer at all! Hallelujah! Now, my question was, what did we see on the CT scan and the PET scan then?

The surgeon told me that they were still going to conduct a culture test for a few more days to complete the 42 days of culturing the sample in order to confirm or to rule out tuberculosis because of the persistent cough which I have had since I was a child.

The church continued to pray and after the completion of 42 days, the consultant called to say that it was not tuberculosis. Another answers to prayers!

According to them, the only thing they had not ruled out by this time, was "Pulmonary Sarcoidosis" but the diagnosis was not conclusive. Even though I was breathless and had rashes even before the day of my admission to hospital, all symptoms had varnished.

I was on steroids prescription for three months to shrink the lymph nodes which could have remained swollen due to the five bouts of chest infections I had the previous year. The doctors could not conclusively diagnose me of any disease, even though they saw many symptoms that could be misleading.

After 6 weeks, I was taken off the steroids because the breathlessness disappeared, the scans showed that the lymph nodes were back to normal size and I was perfectly fine. My lung test was perfect and I was discharged from the clinic officially.

My observation of what I had gone through are that:

Every time they named a disease and booked or started an investigation, the brethren prayed, declared the word, and asked for the quickening of the Holy Spirit. Afterwards, the symptoms and reasons for ordering the investigation just varnished.

As I declared the word daily, the symptoms disappeared and became progressively healed.

"My son, give attention to my words; incline your ear to my sayings. Do not let them

depart from your eyes; keep them in the midst of your heart; for they are life to those who find them, and health to all their flesh."
Proverbs 4:20-22(NKJV)

The word of God gave life and health to my flesh and I was made whole.

God was progressively healing me over a period of six (6) months. He indeed did a "MOT" and drove out all the diseases one after the other. This is to humble me so that I may have no boastings except in the Lord.

For the first five months of these investigations, I was not prescribed any medication or treatment at all, yet the symptoms kept disappearing one after the other.

Even the cough that I had all my life, was gone. I was given a clean bill of health.

There has been no time that I have been glad that I belong to the body of Christ more than this time. The love and sacrifice of the brethren was indeed matchless. God bless you all and all glory be to God!

I do not know what you believe in or what lies that might have been sold to you about divine healing, I confidently know that God heals, because He healed me by His power alone.

"He himself bore our sins in his body on the cross, so that we might die to sins and live for righteousness; by his wounds you have been healed." **1 Peter 2:24(NIV)**

Also in **Romans 8:11(NKJV)**. *But if the Spirit of Him who raised Jesus from the dead dwells in you, He who raised Christ from the dead will also give life to your mortal bodies through His Spirit who dwells in you.*

Begin to declare these words today and His word and His Spirit will heal you just as His word brought healing to my body.

SECTION THREE

"What You Say Is What You Get"

The Shunamite woman in **2 Kings 4:20-26,** left a dead child in the house and went to see the prophet. When asked if all was well, she said in **verse 26** "...*it is well*..." was she lying? NO! she was "faith speaking". What are you saying about your health?

Mark 5:25-28(NKJV) records the account of a certain woman who had a flow of blood for twelve years, she heard about Jesus and came behind him saying "...*If I may touch but his clothes, I shall be well*" **(Mark 5:28)**.

Even Jesus said "*Daughter, your faith has made you whole*" **(Mark 5:34)**. What are you saying about your health?

CHAPTER 9

LIFE IN THE TONGUE

"Death and life are in the power of the tongue, And those who love it will eat its fruit."
Proverbs 18:21(NKJV)

Whatever you give a voice becomes stronger and of course, works for you. During my ordeal, I refused to give the disease a voice, not by denial or secrecy, but by declaring the word of God as an answer to every greeting, question or query.

Whenever I was greeted, "How are you?", I answered, "I am healed by the Lord?"

"How do you feel?" I answered, "I am healed by the Lord" or "quickened by the Spirit." What is the diagnosis? I answered,

"1 Peter 2:24" or **"Isaiah 53:5."**

Some people understood, others laughed, others thought I was becoming crazy or experiencing insanity as the diseases progresses, but I knew that I had to take my healing by force and would not give a voice to the agenda of darkness.

You must of a necessity, declare scriptures when you need healing from the Lord. He will perform His word and it will always fulfil the purpose for which it's been sent.

CHAPTER 10

MAINTAIN YOUR HEALING

"Now it was told the king of Egypt that the people had fled, and the heart of Pharaoh and his servants was turned against the people; and they said, "Why have we done this, that we have let Israel go from serving us?" So he made ready his chariot and took his people with him. Also, he took six hundred choice chariots, and all the chariots of Egypt with captains over every one of them".
Exodus 14:5-6(NKJV)

What a season of supernatural healing, I was once again full of joy that in my life, I have obtained mercy from the Lord. I felt so good with no pain or breathlessness in the body.

I began to share the testimony to Pastors in our region, people in our church and prayer ministry, *"the Lord is good, and His mercy endures for ever".* **Psalm 136:1(NKJV)**

As I read the biblical story of the 10 lepers a few months ago, I was led by the Holy Spirit to do a thanksgiving service and celebration in honour to God for His grace and mercy and to put the account of my ordeal and healing in a book in order to bless people across the world so that they can be enabled to believe God for their own healing. Would it surprise you that as soon as I delivered this book to the publisher, all the symptoms I had in 2019 came back; I became breathless again.

At this point, the scripture at the beginning of this chapter - Exodus 14:5-6, came to mind. It narrated how the Lord had delivered the children of Israel from Pharaoh and the Egyptian slavery; suddenly the Egyptians and Pharaoh realised that the children of Israel were not coming back into slavery, they began to regret letting them go TO WORSHIP GOD;

which was the major reason why they were set free. The reason why God will set you free; the reason why He will heal and deliver you, is **to worship him**.

Luke 1:74-75*(AMPC)* says that God will grant us to be delivered for one reason which is that we *"might serve Him fearlessly in holiness (divine consecration) and righteousness [in accordance with the everlasting principles of right] within His presence all the days of our lives"*

The Lord healed me so that I would serve before Him fearlessly in holiness and righteousness in His presence all the days of my life.

Pharaoh said *"What is this we have done?" why have we let Israel go......?"* This was the same way the enemy began to contend with my healing and freedom. He collaborated with the old symptoms which began to manifest in my body in order to shake my faith and steal my joy.

It was same way, the children of Israel saw the Red Sea and the enemy said to them, *"You are going nowhere"*. The Red Sea at the front, the horses and chariots of the enemy behind pursuing them was an indication of the devil reminding the Israelites about their past in servitude and making them paranoid about their future freedom. What an evil collaboration!

It was more of the enemy saying, "the sea will keep you for us and we will overrun you". The Egyptians pursued relentlessly, but the God of Israel arose and parted the red sea miraculously

This was the enemies' intention for me as well. He wanted me to be afraid. So that I will doubt and begin to question God. He told me "you are going to die" and on the first day after experiencing the symptoms again, I was afraid, not of death but of falling ill as I was the first time.

However, I thank God for the Holy Spirit, my helper, the one who helps our infirmities and comforts us. He encouraged me, reminding me of the faithfulness of God, *whatever God does is forever* (**Ecclesiastes 3:14**)

He reminded me that "...*the word of God is living and powerful....* (**Hebrews 4:12**) and instructed me to stand on the word according to **Mark 11:23** which says *For assuredly, I say to you, whoever says to this mountain, 'Be removed and be cast into the sea,' and does not doubt in his heart, but believes that those things he says will be done, he will have whatever he says.*

I began to speak to and against the symptoms vehemently through the Word of God. I resisted the devil for a couple of days and the symptoms stopped.

The enemy does not want to let go of his captives. After a major breakthrough, he may still pursue again with the intention of the affliction. **Nahum 1:9** says no conspiracy against the Lord will stand and affliction will not rise the second time. This scripture is another anchor of faith. Stand firm in it!

It may even surface as a form of doubt, resist it by speaking to it. Say," I refuse to doubt in the name of Jesus".

When fear comes, resist it by speaking to it. Say it loudly, "I refuse to fear in the name of Jesus".

When sickness comes, resist it by speaking to it. Say confidently, "I refuse sickness in the name of Jesus".

When the old symptoms come back resist it with passion, do it repeatedly, refuse to surrender and by the grace of God, it will go and you shall be delivered.

Here is a suggested confession that will help you keep your healing:

Confession:

In the Name of the Lord Jesus Christ, I exercise authority over my body. I command sickness and disease to leave. I refuse to allow you to stay because my body is the temple for the Holy Spirit.

Satan, you have no right to trespass on God's property. I have authority over you. I know it, you know it, and God knows it. Now, leave my body. I hold fast to what the Lord has done in me and through me. I am healed and I am keeping my healing in Jesus Christ.

Repeat this confession until you get it into your spirit. Refuse to succumb to the devil and its tricks.

In case you have read this book and you do not know the Lord intimately or have missed your way or straying away from him, you can come to the Lord today and you will receive healing that is meant for his children **(Matthew 15:26)**

Here is what to do:

1. Confess your sins
2. Pray as follows:

Dear Heavenly Father,

I come to You today with my hearts wide open. I confess that I have rejected you and lived my life on my own terms. I acknowledge that I am a sinner in need of the Saviour.

I call upon the name of your dear son, Jesus Christ, that I might be saved.

You have said, "that if you confess with your mouth the Lord Jesus and believe in your heart that God has raised Him from the dead, you will be saved. For with the heart one believes unto righteousness, and with the mouth confession is made unto salvation" **Romans. 10:9, 10(NKJV).**

I believe in my heart that Jesus Christ is the Son of God. I believe that He lived here on earth, died and was raised from the dead for my justification, and I confess Him now as my Lord.

Lord Jesus, I invite you to come into my life, be my Lord and personal Saviour. I surrender all to you, take full control of my life. Thank you Lord, I am saved

3. Now that you are saved, please find a Bible believing church near you to attend so you can grow and be supported in your journey of faith.

If you said this prayer for the first time or re-dedicated your life to Christ, please send an email to prayer@toyintaiwo.org for further prayers.

CHAPTER 11

AND THEN SOME……

HEALING SCRIPTURES

Luke 6:19 – **And** the people all tried to touch him, because power was coming from him and healing them all.

Isaiah 57:18-19 – I have seen their ways, but I will heal them; I will guide them and restore comfort to Israel's mourners, creating praise on their lips. "Peace, peace, to those far and near," says the Lord, "And I will heal them."

1 Peter 2:24 – He himself bore our sins in his body on the cross, so that we might die to sins and live for righteousness; by his wounds you have been healed.

Psalms 107:20-21 – He sent out his word and healed them; he rescued them from the grave. Let them give thanks to the Lord for his unfailing love and his wonderful deeds for mankind.

Psalms 147:3 – He heals the broken hearted and binds up their wounds.

Jeremiah 17:14 – Heal me, Lord, and I will be healed; save me and I will be saved, for you are the one I praise.

Exodus 23:25 – Worship the LORD your God, and his blessing will be on your food and water. I will take away sickness from among you.

Matthew 15:13 – Jesus replied, "Every plant not planted by my heavenly Father will be uprooted.

3 John 1:2 – Beloved, I pray that all may go well with you and that you may be in good health, as it goes well with your soul.

Psalm 6:2 - Have mercy on me, LORD, for I am faint; heal me, LORD, for my bones are in agony.

Jeremiah30:17a – For I will restore health to you, And heal you of your wounds, 'says the Lord.'

Proverbs 4:20-22 - My son, give attention to my words; incline your ear to my sayings. Do not let them depart from your eyes; keep them in the midst of your heart; for they are life to those who find them, and health to all their flesh.

Isaiah 38:16a - You restored me to health and let me live

Malachi 4:2a – But for you who fear My name, the sun of righteousness shall rise with healing in its wings. You shall go out leaping like calves from the stall.

Romans 8:11 – But if the Spirit of Him who raised Jesus from the dead dwells in you, He who raised Christ from the dead will also give life to your mortal bodies through His Spirit who dwells in you.

Go ahead and declare these word of God over your life. According to **James 4:7** "Resist the devil" afflicting your body or mind and "he will flee from you."

EPILOGUE

There is a lot of people within the body of Christ having sicknesses and diseases in their bodies and in as much as one cannot claim that there is a formula that works, we can surely remind ourselves of the fact that It is God's will to heal, he has promised healing in his word as one of the benefits of the cross and that you can be healed.

The just shall live by faith the bible says I am hopeful that my personal testimonies of healing will inspire you, strengthen your faith and enable you to keep on holding on to God. I want you to know that I am alive by God's grace. It is His mercies that has kept me thus far, not because I'm more worthy or deserving than others in a similar situation who didn't make it but because of his grace and loving kindness.

The aim of this book is to build up our faith in the healing power of God, so that we can lay claim to our divine healing which concluded over 2000 years ago on the cross of Calvary

Keep holding on! Don't give up! God loves you and He is not through with you yet.

ABOUT THE AUTHOR

Toyin Taiwo is the Senior Pastor of Grace Chapel Chesterfield, a growing multicultural church in the town of Chesterfield UK.

She graduated from Bible College in 1996 and she has been in ministry since then. She is a sound teacher of the Word. Through her cutting edge revelations and divine instructions in admonishing others to apply simple biblical principles, the lives of many have been impacted

Her ministry is characterized by her compassionate and loving heart, which makes her to frequently intercede for people, cities, and nations.

Her pastoral heart has empowered her commitment to this sacrificial call upon her life. She is passionate about bringing the Grace of God unto everyone, reaching and making disciples of all mankind with the Good News of Jesus Christ; regardless of race, social or economic status.

Toyin is committed to changing the world one person at a time and to seeing "the church" (Christ's Body) grow and produce true Christians that will light up the world by exceptional Christian living.

Toyin is well known as an international public speaker in conferences, seminars, and leadership trainings all over Europe and North America. Through her prophetic declarations across the nations, lives have been changed and transformed by the power of God.

She is married to Debo Taiwo and they are blessed with children.

OTHER BOOKS

This book is an anointed manual with the capacity of reviving any Christian who is in a dry place or wants to go to the next level in intimacy with Christ in 21 days. It can be used for personal daily prayers, in groups or in retreats.

This book was written out of an experience of 365 days of speaking in tongues and listening to God, submitting to His will and obeying Him.

It is an anointed prayer devotional with the capacity to renew and revive any Christian who desires a consistent walk with God or desires next level of intimacy with Christ in 365 days.

The book is borne out of several meetings and LIVE experiences through which many have received the baptism and gifts of the Holy Spirit.

After this experience, lives have been changed ministries and callings have been birthed, threshing floor has been cleared, making room for God's manifestation in their lives. Also, other facets of life were attended to bring all round healing and health

You can order these books from toyintaiwo.org or from Amazon.

BIBLIOGRAPHY

- Enduring Word Commentary - online
- The Healing Line by Grace M Sarber
- Battlefield of The Mind by Joyce Meyer
- Choosept.com - online

NOTES

Printed in Great Britain
by Amazon